Ayo Ayo Ayo and Other Love Songs

by

Moses Kainwo

ISBN: 978-99910-54-001

Sierra Leonean Writers Series

&

Karantha Publishers

Dedication

The outings that birthed the poetry walkabouts
A little light here
A little madness there
Even when in name only
Falui takes the name
But when in blame only
Falui should not take the blame
So Falui Poetry Society
I give this back to you

Acknowledgment

We ate stories round the night fires
On top of roasted cassava in palm oil
At the end of the farm day
With only one *chef*
Ngɔ Miata—my mother

She remained silent to my love appeals
In those love letters
As if she didn't care
So I wrote more just to fetch a bird's peck
Violet—my wife

The genius in them—in the evenings
Forced out new theatricals at home
Without prompters from a living backstage
Of the day and of the times
Jeelo and Jeeta—my daughters

Contents

Love as Continuum of Communion

Book Endorsements

The poet skillfully uses metaphor and symbolism to describe real life situations and contemporary issues in poetic format. The images he chooses, forceful, hone home his thoughts on a wide range of subjects in a concise, crisp and terse manner that holds the reader spell bound as he goes through the collection of poems. The poet has broken new ground in Sierra Leone's contemporary literature.

--Bernadette Cole, Immediate past Dean, Faculty of Arts, Fourah Bay College

****

An utterly beguiling collection, a new voice buried in tested wisdom. Moses Kainwo's poems successfully experiment with different forms of designs in content and in art. At its core, *Ayo Ayo Ayo* deals with the bittersweet memories of war from which a fruitcake of love emerges 'from wounds of a heart'.

--Gbanabom Hallowell, Director, SLBC

Goombay for Kainwo

Out of the bulls
Eye of the bush
Buffalo's heart
Land, drum
Beats burst—a
Blaze.

Some awe
Some, awe-inspiring
Phenomenon of taut
Talking tom
Toms a
Boil with hot iron
Tongues of fire—

Forest deep
Vocables of a sac
Red, bearded
Bard with indelible
Oracles on the back
Side of his face—a

Lights with dazzling
Cadence and dance, like
Izzards of
Unquenchable thunder
Bolts, on the
Tympanum of our
Nation in the doldrums

Kicks in a quick
Tick into our toes
Zippy up the
Pelvis to our back
Bones and then
Breaks
Out of bone
Marrows with one
Cracking carnival a

Cross the country

Rev Ambrose Massaquoi
Principal/Poet
Africa Centre for Theological Studies, Lagos,
Nigeria

Kainwo's Love Songs depict a deep and emotional sense of now and the thereafter. The imagery of these poems covers every aspect of life; the casual, the serious and the spiritually uplifting. I have read many of Kainwo's unpublished works. The choice for this volume is a true blend of his range of styles and subjects. He weaves these in verses depicting war and suffering, love and misfortune, poverty and freedom. We are introduced to Kainwo's direct-indirect repetitive style which he uses to convey emphasis.

In some of the poems, he gives us an imaginative commentary on characters revered and others loathed. His letters to Mandela and Corporal Foday Sankoh, make contrasts in powerful metaphors:

In Mandela we have the verses:
You know
> All life in him
> All light in him
> All present in him
> All future in him.

In the letter to Foday Sankoh, the difference is unambiguously clear. He states his inner revulsion to his atrocities. Here we read:
> innocent blood queries my throat
> please field marshal
> president of another world.
> chief justice of injustice
> hold.

What is striking about this collection is that it covers areas of human experience that stir up emotions at various levels of sadness, regret and hope. In 'The Seasons' we see the transition of all these as the seasons change. Such masterly construction of the stanzas is repeated in other poems. There are poems of human love and godliness, which relieve the strong expressions of calamity in poems like 'Sallay Kama Salla' and the awareness and defiance in the verses on AIDS. But there is surprise and coincidence in the poems on 'Letters to..' Again, the imaginative and expressive Kainwo, shows up touching sensitive nerves and drawing the reader to experience the deep feelings in these messages.

Ayo Ayo Ayo Ayo, sets the story of Sierra Leone's journey from independence to its jubilee year, in blank verse. This is a tale of despair and hope. I consider this a companion piece to the poem, 'The Salone Leone of the Seventies;' nostalgic in part and as damming as Kainwo's use of elegant imagery could portray. As a theologian, it is not surprising that the author draws inspiration from characters in the scriptures. Great authors have based their poems on well known characters from history. Tennyson, for example uses characters from Greek mythology in his poems 'Ulysses' and 'Tithonus'. Kainwo's religious characters are brought into secular light. He makes them refreshingly real, in the context of their biblical reputations.

Kainwo's Love Songs is a unique addition to the growing number of Sierra Leonean writings.
The songs don't sing,
But the words speak from the heart.

K. Koso-Thomas
Writer and Painter

Foreword

The marriage of poetry and religion is probably best remembered when one thinks of the career of the English poet-priest Gerald Manley Hopkins. Although many of this shy poet's verses were published only after his death, his influence on Middle English and Modern English poetry was quite significant. His simplicity and striking imagery, no doubt derived from the austere and restrictive life of a priest, were of a beauty and richness not too common in those days. Moreover, in trying to understand him, readers were quite aware of his personal life's struggles, his self doubt and sexual anguish; all of which he tried to subdue with admirable courage. But the nineteenth century England of Hopkins was a much different place from the contemporary settings of the poetry of another poet-pastor, Moses Kainwo. If Manley Hopkins's England was mostly rural it was at least peaceful, if somewhat archaic in verse and outlook.

The Sierra Leone of Moses Kainwo's poetry, on the other hand, is a completely different world from that of the English ascetic. Nor for that matter did Hopkins experience the horrific tragedies of war and death that Kainwo lived through. A sense of betrayal, especially by those in whom trust was placed, is not what poets usually want to experience. But in Kainwo's case, it was part of the template: humanity suffered deeply from a cruel abandonment of that most basic of values in Sierra Leone: decency! So it is even more surprising that, out of that sense of betrayal and horror, so much poetry has come from a new generation of Sierra Leonean poets, the majority of whom are either in their late forties or early fifties. Moses Kainwo is one such poet.

In reading him, I find it difficult to make the distinction between whether his poetry is propelled simply by a deep sense of religious love of people and country, or by the understandable anguish suffered by a poet of deep compassion over the recent tragedies in his homeland.

For, in a sense, the waging of war, at least from the point of view of some of its protagonists, is as much a religious fiat as it is political. And in using religion to understand the morality, or injustice, of war, Kainwo does not make it easy for us to choose.

One thing is clear though: these are poems from a man of unquestioned hope and humanity. From the landscape of war he has crafted some soaring and beautiful lines that are deeply spiritual as well as political in tone.

Kainwo is keenly aware of history. Or, rather, what Sierra Leoneans have done to the history of a country. In his poems, one does not read about the presumed 'greatness' of a past, but of the neglect of that past; a transition from the kindness and mortality of man/ woman to the wantonness of the crazed and monstrous. Like most men of reason, the poet finds it hard to understand how a nation could have descended into the kind of anarchy that so savagely consumed us in the recent past. But like all good poets and clergymen, it is his duty to both reflect on the tragedy and to hope for some form of redemption from the greed and wantonness responsible for that tragedy.

So, in the poem *forgiveness,* the poet reminds us that we are all casualties; that there are no saints and sinners.

Forgiven—I have been forgiven.
To forgive—let me be a giver,
And to give—let me be a loser,
And to lose—let me be a winner.

In the poem *God Is Posh,* Kainwo continues his probing of the true meaning of God in all of us. If the name (idea) of God is about a moral quest for some of us, then what about those who have committed horrific crimes in his name? The poet seems to be asking!

There are other religious poems of touching simplicity and beauty: those in which readers of varying tastes and pleasures will find their souls or comfort. Some are exaltations; while others are, in a sense, simply spiritual.

There are poems of war: specifically, poems addressed to the perpetrators of war; such as the rebel chieftain Foday Sankoh. Then there are the love poems to his daughter and her cat: these are very touching and beautiful. And in another love poem, *No Need To Say Farewell,* the poet seems to be telling his readers how hard it is to say goodbye to a loved one.

And, of course, as a good student of the history of our beautiful but troubled continent, there are poems to the nobility of a giant like Nelson Mandela and to the heroism of the captives on the Amistad.

Love, death, war, benediction and salvation: you will find plenty of these in Moses Kainwo's poems. He is not an ascetic like Gerald Manley Hopkins, nor do I have the impression that his poetry has come from a long period of self doubt and the renouncement of basic pleasures. But there is no doubt that pain has touched this poet. From that deep reservoir of suffering, he has reached out to all the casualties of not just the problems in his homeland, but beyond. Like all good poets, he has cast his lenses on all humanity, as in these lines taken from his poem addressed to the victims of the Katrina disaster in New Orleans.

Beware Honey
Bells of night may ring again
To wake the sleepers of day
If only they can rise from sleep

With this volume, Kainwo has helped to awaken the bones of the philistines and taken his place amongst the most promising of the new generation of Sierra Leonean poets.

Professor Syl Cheney-Coker
Poet
Author of *The Road to Jamaica* (SLWS 2015)

Introduction

Love is perhaps the most misunderstood, most desired, most perfect imperfection of all the human emotions. And by the time one reaches middle-age, it's recognized that to know the truth of love, one must have seen and held loss.

Moses Kainwo's poems acknowledge the duplicity of such depth of feeling, for oneself, for one's family, for one's country, and within his poems the images are witnesses that do not attempt to explain or answer, but rather, recognize.

What remains in the postscript of devastating war? Loss is visible in every broken house and body, the scars on the land, and the fissures in a government. But again, what remains? More than emptiness? We save what we can, we look for what's left.

Can every single part of a person, of a country, be killed? It's a question Kainwo poses throughout, and in his concrete poem "Can You Kill Me" that moves visually and verbally like wind, pushing and pulling at memory, at bad and good intentions, resolves with the most profound of answers: "my spirit goes on/i must go on".

Jubilee and war stand next to each other, straight-backed and full of power, yet in opposing ways. The charge, then, becomes one of harnessing the power, letting go of the kind that hurts, embodying the kind that strengthens the soul.

The poems in this collection in some ways breathe forgiveness, unafraid to look honestly or to acknowledge the pain and hard changes that memory insists on maintaining; and in doing so, allow courage to not turn away to allow the light to seep through the cracks. The human spirit of survival, of family, and yes, of love, to be what remains. Still.

These are poems of resilience. They are the geography of beginnings and endings, they are letters to a younger generation born after the war, and they are love letters to those who lived through it. In reading Kainwo's words, a kind of belief is restored, necessary, and assumptive of goodness. What else could there possibly be to stitch together the past and the present? To survive? To find the grace amidst its seeming absence? The stories in these poems are evidence, they are learned truths, they are love.

--Kirsten Rian, writer, USA

Love in Time of War

Battle Talk

Advance
According to formation
And chop them up
While you lose

Retreat
According to plan
And give them up
While you win

Amistad![1]

Punches thrown for man and country
      Punches gotten for man and woman
            What they did we did in Amistad
  Yes… punches… for women and children
Take it so… for man and country

What a way for fettered friendships
      Given or thrown for man and country
          Taken or laid by hands in Amistad
      Redundant aches for man and country
You and I… amid star judges forever

Sails mounted on the Atlantic Ocean
      Are a famished embodiment
          Of love and hate in Amistad
      Souls neither blue nor white
Are sailing… sailing… sailing…

Yet they come from careless neglect
  Sons and daughters of Chiefs and Queens
      With no names from more names in Amistad
      So I salute with enthusiasm
My siblings who sail on the seas

---

[1] *La Amistad* is the name of a Spanish slave ship associated with the mutiny of Sierra Leonean slaves off the coast of the USA in 1839. In Spanish the word Amistad means friendship.

Guilty punches thrown by Malice
      Sengbe Pieh[2] is a better name
         And a Monarch gave birth to Amistad
   Sengbe whose blood knows how to spell **NO**
With echoes on land and sea

And what he did I truly did
      I got back my soul from punches
          Amistad Friendship Amistad
    Blast many horns for many ears
That the children may hear and live

But from what you say you have not heard
     From what you do you have not heard
       From what you see there is no Amistad
   So Amistad horns will keep blasting
For those of us that have not heard

Amistad! Friendship! Amistad! Friendship! Amistad!
Friendship! Amistad!

---

[2] Sengbe Pieh was the original name of the man who spearheaded the revolt on the ship in 1839 but officially called Joseph Cinque.

I Can Feel Your Pulse from Here

I can feel your pulse from here:
The watchman for Flee-Town.
I sat in the pinnacle
And saw the ants (black and white)
Streaming towards the city.

Here too I am my nation:
A piece of your earthly dream,
The necklace for poor neighbours,
And they say, "Come on boy,
A piece of you will feed us".

O they won't care to know you,
Where they don't care to see you:
They say your streets are too red,
With sexless ageless lifeblood;
I can feel your pulse from here.

Here in the tower I stand,
Standby being my daily bread:
No omolankays,[3] it seems,
Salute me as a chieftain;
But I feel your pulse from here.

Peace has always been my lot:
My teeth know no stream of tears,
Though my eyes keep pouring rains,

---

[3] Omolankay: A push cart used to transport goods mostly in the cities of
Sierra Leone.

7

And nameless drops anoint my heart,
Leaving there emotion drops.

Before me the projects rise:
Before me the poor are sliced,
I am butchered left and right,
For the sake of jewelry,
That lie so close to my heart.

Let someone hear my dreaming,
For caring gents and ladies:
That each may bear the nation,
In the watchtower for Flee-Town,
As I feel your pulse from here.

My tears are named as naked,
Each time each drops on air;
They wet my heart with stories,
Untold where God has ground;
But I feel your pulse from here.

On the Screen

On the screen:
I saw famine stricken lands
And a girl dying—
Not from food famine,
But from family famine;
No family member was there
To open the door...

And then on the screen:
I saw war-stricken lands
And a boy soldier dying
Not from gunshot wounds
But from wounds of a heart
That would not part with a father
Whose grave was too raw...

Yet still on the screen:
The great killer breeze, in one clenched call,
Sent thousands to hell:
For being too slow,
Too slow for the heavenly chariot;
And they managed to pray,
"God, why do you forsake ..."

And we all sat there,
Double-breasted,
With snobbish teeth and tears,
And the question,
"Who would go for us?"
Was answered with enthusiasm,
"The Seventh World Saviours!"

A Letter to Mr Nelson Mandela: 11th February, 1990

Once in
Some in you go in with you
  Your self
  Your family
  Your land
  Complaining with you

Once out
Some in you come out with you
  Your self
  Your family
  Your land
  Forgiving with you

One thing
  Yet knows no suffering
  Knows no boundaries
  Whether in or out of holes
  Is your voice crowned

You know
  All life in him
  All light in him
  All present in him
  All future in him

Standing free
  In your black
  In your white
  In your family

In your land
Saves the land

So, brother, hold on!

A Letter to Corporal Foday Sankoh[4]

dear mr sun-core

hold and let the handshake speak
i know your lenses are blind to kailondo's[5] staff
i know your wavelength is deaf to kailondo's voice
but hold

innocent blood queries my throat
please field marshal
president of another world
chief justice of injustice
hold

touch wood
that you would grant the insane your sanity
the cocoa your freedom
the unborn your hope

please mr sun-core
hold
and let the handshake speak

---

[4] Corporal Foday Sebana Sankoh was the name of the man who led the rebels of Sierra Leone in the eleven-year old war (1991 – 2002).

[5] Kailondo was a famous Mende warrior from the East of Sierra Leone.

The Culture of Peeping

1.   Eyes

I

The young are short-sighted from seeing too much,
The old are long-sighted from seeing so much.
Children peep to see with elderly eyes
Dancing adults in their love store and cries.

See them now blinking at photos at play,
While adults must blink their fanlight replay:
The ticklish world will unlock a window,
The greedy world will shut the gazer's show.

Little surprise some shutters are so thick,
Though lucent curtains serve the purpose pick:
Many a gazer will tick to street bells,
And choose not to be their sisters' angels.

II

Oh yes you can choose to see or not see,
Because death standing in that deafening knell,
Attracts a witness that is not witness:
Behind the window blinds the conscience stress.

I turned it on my mind over again,
Me too, I am not my sister's bargain;
I am her Lucifer[6] to chant her there,
And since no one beholds I shall not care.

---

[6] Lucifer is another name for Satan, the fallen angel (See Isaiah 14:12).

14

Lucifer is in you my country bore:
Together we mused and our sister tore,
From the Gallery down to the Crypt,
And from the Crypt down into the street.

If by this token new perception drops,
Then the nation wins the cowering crops:
Elect a hoodlum and you have an imp,
There you'll survive with a well-earned gimp.

Let each goggle gauge a reverse gazing,
On the battered soul deformed from blazing:
Indeed a sorry darkness sits within,
And only when it rises will it spin.

2.   **Rivers**

I

Five great rivers the death comrades did cross,
To square up with the age-old peeping loss:
They broke the bridges and co-steered their way,
The strange navigators driven by pay.

An evening salute from death on the streets,
Was not so welcome to the peeping feet;
In fact the streets died with a woeful woe,
As they bled and wasted before the foe.

Their names were written in the book of pyres,
To choose their deaths in the face of hellfire:
They received the eye-bursting-dripping beads,

Or the gift of shirts with chosen sleeves.

New rivers began to flow the main roads,
Nameless rivers made of countless red loads:
My sister peeped and her eyes became blood,
Her letter of love was there in the flood.

II

Operation-no-living-thing had no date,
But this poetaster hit the tape
Before Death sharpened the machete and cursed,
And there blood flowed for the nursed to swim.

No one ever cursed like that heavyweight,
No one ever cried like that featherweight;
The two looked at each other in the eye,
And the new peeping game was cast in dye.

But there was no rhythm in the new song:
By the Atlantic Ocean there we sat up,
Waiting for a boat to sail or fly,
Anywhere on God's good terrain to swarm.

The river flowed on flora and fauna,
Shoppers jumping on to Noah's basket:
Some green some white some blue unseemly queues,
Singing how we exhaust God in the blues.

One mosquito that sucked the blood,
And became fat and burst open with flood:
Was rotten and not good for washing,
So it was drained and bottled in a sink.

3.   Creation

Was this the way the universe began,
Or is it where the universe will dance,
In green and white and blue of any shape,
With lions unseen on mountains in cape?

The metaphysics of the guessed order,
Throws naiveté at the vexed founder:
And that imaginative family tree,
Is god-planted to harbour fleas.

The Cotton Tree of Flee-town is like a god,
Around whom the fleas converge day and night;
And every sober march re-routes from there,
So she is amply fed and dressed right there.

Where the green god stands there is flesh on bones,
There is hope on toes that the green god knows,
From daybreak to nightfall they come and go,
Lifting new symbols from the place below.

Not one burgher knows who proscribed with fire,
And I want to ask who lighted the tyre.
Who made the bad heart, I can only guess?
But who declared the war we should not now stress.

How can we know where knowledge is remote?
You press a knob and something is afloat,
You lift a finger and some figure drowns;
The bluecoat is there with his fingers cupped.

They say the Cotton Tree saw them chop dogs,
She must have also seen them bogging bogs.

But who can make her tell the faded tale,
When the truth itself has been painted pale?

The sold train track some travel curses banned,
The power now rests in the palm of the band,
This also is now in the poda handout;
But real power remains in the poda rear mouth.

Right around your base and just yesterday,
America waved in the nude by day;
And again yesterday like the other judge,
UNAMSIL[7] was baptizing in the lodge.

And they said, "disrobe to enter the pond!".
He took off a shirt and then the bell-bottoms:
Four shirts and four trousers on one body,
A moving wardrobe in fear of war folly.

Story-telling Tree, receive the prayers,
Given in jest as a test of the years,
Your children will come from obloquy and cry,
Forgive their past and from your glory spy.

You gave them a tongue and gave them a song,
You gave them the drug and gave them the time,
The chequered love of a chequered nation,
But the wheat and the tares must have options.

4.   Seasons

The dries are not summer so call them that,
Winter and autumn each have their own flag;

---

[7] UNAMSIL: United Nations Mission in Sierra Leone

They will come next year and always be first,
But will not spring where the reason is wet.

The tears in you will come as will the rain,
Because the soul is alive with the times,
And the charred remnants of battle will float,
To announce the evidence of battered throat.

And one drunken gun-totter said to me,
"This is your own ambush brave pedigree,
Empty your pockets on a deserving angel,
The revolution is here first to sell".

"Was this the accord you promised to pour,
Hunger and thirst rained upon all the poor?"
I could not ask more that desperado—
The stooge of death ordered the thing to do.

Someone will hate the success tale you tell,
Someone will speak black spittle at your wealth;
But please succeed and retreat from the rest,
To hold onto excess will be a test.

Can present time annul past time and stay?
You cannot bat the ball and keep it—nooooo!
The aged say the times are new to them,
The young reckon but say their time is tame.

We don't even know who last left the shores,
Since the going is similar to coming.
Can you actually blame the move on one,
When in your heart of hearts you hate the one?

To appear they had to disappear,
But time will come though time is always here;
And time once lost is time forever gone,
The time will come and they indeed will come.

Roses stand in dustbins that they may smell sweet,
We need one on this ground for wiping feet:
Life now smells of the swift and the ugly,
Any revolution will make the foolish champion.

Can You Kill Me?

can you kill me

tear my flesh apart
    smash my brain out
        use a bomb
           or a missile
        or a gun
    or a rope
   or an arrow
or a cutlass
my voice bears children of my kind
my song moves quicker on their lips
they bear grandchildren

my spirit goes on
i must go on

Kitana My Daughter's Cat

Kitana my daughter's tomcat
Goes to school to practise to play
His new-tamed paws will march in a house
Rather than mow down a mouse

All day long he will twist his tongue
To chitchat on the Queen's blue tongue
The rats and mice will sway their tails
With Kitana so hot on their trail

The teacher once voted a verse
But Kitana reversed for a dash
In a window had sat a rat
An offence to my daughter's cat

He went for the hind of his find
The kind that satisfied his mind
He had gone to school on a fast
But now had a find for breakfast

Kitana Kitana they yelled
As children and teacher beheld
A bully had come to their school
And had no regard for the rules

Kitana was thrown out of school
For conduct that questioned the rules
So he went to court with his tail
To win back his name from their tale

The lady judge sat on dried rat
With table well made from dried fish
Vermin skin veiled all the windows
For fear of the street in shadows

Kitana your case you may state
The judge in her seat did dictate
Kitana licked his paws from the dock
In a bid to defend his frock

Kitana spoke in Queen's blue tongue
Though hungry he stood there for long
He told of the degradation
The teacher had made his portion

The judge adjourned for five minutes
In which time her table diminished
Kitana with table in mouth
Disappeared from court without doubt

He never returned to the school
He never returned to be ruled
The judge so surprised did not fight
With case and table out of sight

Kitana was no more in sight
Not in school nor in dock nor in sight
But Police dogged him with their dog
That never returned from the dream

The Rare Rulers

As if the people are paper
They rule with a ruler
  The gun as red-ink pen
  Thunders decrees from dawn to dusk
  And the people become paper

Yet I never knew
Could never guess
The skull of humans could be cup
Of lasting thought score in the hand

And the cup too is a ruler
Where the people play stiff before it
And spread like paper to be ruled

The rulers lie straight
Like snakes among the people
And writers who drop their mixture of ink
On the bodies of rulers
Will instantly change their house address

I Must Rise, Bathsheba[8]

I must rise to see
The shadow or shape
I need to rise
Straighten my neck
And slap the air
On tiptoe—I must rise

Should I call her
To see me rise
Again and again
Should she tempt me
Or should I tempt her
I will tempt her—on tiptoe

On this rooftop
I don't need a bed or do I
For that shadow do I
I will baptize her
Again and again
On tiptoe—when I rise

Should I play the harp
For that shape
Will she break or dance
For my heart
Will she take my heart
If I give her—on tiptoe

---

[8] Bathsheba: The name of the woman whom King David seduced in the
Bible (See 2 Samuel 11:3).

I dare erase it all
The thought after the act
That is after rising
To view the stream
And the shape or shadow
After rising—on tiptoe

I Have Rights, David[9]

I chased and took rights
And can give rights I bet
I dare give rights
To power balls
Or be crushed
Under rights—on my bot

Rights to the stream or river or beach
To give my looks
To the wind on site
For site seeing
On my feet—for a bath
I have rights—to my bot

I cherish rights
Human or animal rights
To stretch my legs
In exercise—to bend down
With my shape
On my feet or bottom—all my rights

My rights are mine
By the stream or water well
In the day or in the night
On my feet or bottom
To clap my shadow—in exercise
I take rights—where I can

---

[9] David: Famous king in the Bible reputed to have written most of the Psalms.

Take the rights I give
In faithful or faithless jokes
In the day or in the night
At your house or at my house
On the rooftop—with no bed

It is mine to give—if you dare take

Letters

a letter sealed
is a bomb concealed
inside is action sentence
covered with innocence

on breaking through
it does you
and you leap
or fall
or scatter

it speaks life or death
better than a silent messenger
who staggers for breath

Savage or Garbage

Call me a savage
But give me a chance
To grow like you
And be some garbage

The Vote Against AIDS[10]

Our vote for ill health
Is a vote for world death
Our vote supporting AIDS
Is in aid of full hell

Our vote against ill health
Is a vote for world health
Our vote against AIDS
Is in aid of full wealth

Where we pledge for world health

---

[10] AIDS: Acquired Immuno Deficiency Syndrome

Stony AIDS

A battle to fight
A war to win
with stones
dead stones
living stones
In your hands
And in my hands too

A very hard stone
A healing stone
Of AIDS
In AIDS
With AIDS
Has killed the virus
And the world is healed

I carried the virus
When I carried the stigma
So positive
So activist
So upbeat
Against you brother
And yet it was I who died

When I dropped the stigma
I dropped the virus
So positive
So activist
So upbeat
In support of you sister
And I'm so much alive

The Sun

Big bang born
Big bang giving
To those who care
For a rise in the morning

The sun will indeed rise
For those who care and for those that don't
The sun will intrude from the horizon
With a smile of hope

There Is a Turning in the Road

There is a turning in the road, traveller;
For a willing, courageous and tested flier.

If you must turn to the left of the road,
Do so knowing the world condemns your code.

If you must turn to the right of the same,
Do so knowing that the world takes no blame.

If you must make an about face turn there,
Do so as a traveller who knows the fare.

But if you must move on on that same road,
Move, o willing, courageous and tested code.

Lebanon on the Move
(To Kitty Fadlu-Deen)

Tantrums from the valley beneath
Are echoed repeatedly from above
If only
If only they'd retreat
Like Kingdom forces
With banner before missile
> You know
> Real peace
> Slipped through their fingers
> Like water in a sieve

Abess Alie-Samir[11] Esquire
Former diamond magnet
I salute you
Did I hear well
That one missile sent you home
To the Bacar Valley
Only for another to send you home
To the *Kambui Hills[12]*

Little did I guess
The conversion of a hilly life
Into a richer valley life
Was an empty vessel
In the hands of choice and duress

---

[11] Abess Alie-Samir: A made-up Lebanese name
[12] *Kambui Hills* is a range of hills surrounding Kenema Town, the town where diamonds are bought and sold in Sierra Leone.

I must add a tear
To your river of tears
In the tearing of a valley
Now seated on the epicentre
Of an earthquake
Measured since 1947
I see your face among the displaced
The dispossessed

When will a ruby stand
In that valley
To salute your signature in style
When will the history book
Be ready for your eyes
When will the children
Recite the verses of Omar Khayyam[13]
When will a President truly say
They gave you a plot
To plot your peace
When will rhetoric grant you
Permission to look at your gems

Maybe soon maybe not
Maybe the tears will dry up
Soon yes very very soon
Let us keep that
They say after dark the dawn
Let us keep that
They say the shadows of moonlight
Will roam and find rest
Let us keep that

---

[13] Omar Kayam: Famous Lebanese poet

They say the shadows under the rubble
May not occur twice
Let us keep that
Or may they

A Flood from the Sky
(In memory of the war on Lebanese soil)

A flood was poured from the sky
Against the will of God
Against the will of man
Except that supermen
Superimposing their flags
Ordered a rain without a rainbow

The urge to move was strong
Against the will of God
Against the will of man
But the woman with a baby inside her
With a brain inside his head
Ordered them to wait

The waiting could be worth it
In the will of God
In the will of man
For in the history of that place
And on the table of that grave
Grave things are measured

In that same place a people were planted
In the will of God
In the will of man
And God the gardener named a garden
With flowers for them to name
If they did there could be no death

In that same place a tree was fixed
With shiny fruit
For the gardener's pleasure
But they claimed the fruit
And changed the truth
So the war threw bones apart

See how innocence is paraded
In the streets of guilt
Against the will of God
Against the will of man
But Hope now holds a lighted lamp
For they will lose the war to God

The intangible flood of love
Is everyone's dream
In the will of God
In the will of man
And this will once restored
Will will the much wished for rainbow

Snap Noise
(After a road accident along Kissy Street renamed Sani Abacha Street)

Three tiers of noise
caught me from the side

one from under the trailer
and on its hind
a carpet for the wheels
as they crushed the madman's legs
while he hung on to the side
of the long mirror-less lorry

the other just behind me
and beside Gibraltar Church
a woman who said
"i am a mother he surely has a mother"
then she cried but continued home

the third from the third floor
a Lebanese peeped and cried
"some relation of his will come
and claim insurance on the lorry"
with his eyes containing the container

So the lorry stopped
To give madness a ride

The Enigma of a Cross

Tell me,
What is a cross?

Is it white, is it black,
Is it white and black?

Is it a feeling in the head, is it a feeling in the skin,
Is it a feeling in the head and skin?

Is it a tree with healing branches, is it a tree with no healing
branches,
Is it a tree with healing and no healing branches all at once?

Is it for a sane man, is it for a man not sane,
Is it for the sane and insane all at once?

Is it a symbol for one God, is it a symbol for many gods,
Is it a symbol for one and many gods all at once?

When America parades, put it before me,
When Africa parades, put it before me.

In the evening put it between the sky and me,
Let its shadow fall on the sky and me.

My eyes should see that cross which they sing about,
That cross, which they talk about.

My hands should touch that cross, which has nail marks;
That cross, which has rope marks.

If this table and this paper and this pen are crosses,

Tell me—so I know I have a cross.

If this country and this leader and these friends are crosses,
Tell me—so I know I have a cross.

If this meeting is a cross,
Tell me—so I know I have a cross.

What is a cross?
Only tell me.

Borders of Truth

Every nation has its moments for expressing ignorance. This nation has chosen this moment to express it in her own nuance. But when History judges this moment, may it never be mentioned of me that I was among those who betrayed the nation. Let me be named among those men and women who crossed over the borders of doubt to the expanse of sanity, who kept the nation going until she arrived at her moment of enlightenment. When that moment comes may my soul be called back from the confines of the grave to dance on the new esplanade of truth.

What, then, Is Scholarship Crowned?

what, then, is scholarship crowned?

yes, yes, a voice —
a voice with limbs
of a full-grown man
impaired

when crowned by tongue,
he debits the world their right to speeches,
and their voices drown.

when crowned by limbs,
he debits the world their right to labour,
and their actions drown.

when crowned by head,
he debits the world their right to silence,
and their persons rise.

yet the critics fall together,
laughing out their heads:
"i wish it were not written,
i wish it were not spoken";
and the timid fall together,
weeping out their heads:
"i wish I had not written,
i wish I had not spoken".

sold!

Ceasefire

Cease!
The fire eats you,
The fire eats them.

Peace!
It must cost you,
It must cost them.

Build!
The work calls you,
The work calls them.

Peace Talk

Mr. Prime Minister, Mr. President,
I am your President.

My name is Abraham, your father;
I love my family—as your father.

Jews, can you see me?
Arabs, can you see me?

Your peace is my peace!
Your pain is my pain!

Warn your children,
Not to go behind me.

Hatred is on my back,
Poverty is on my back.

My Wish List

That I may vote the ordinary
Every day
In spite of the extra-ordinary

That I may see my epitaph in preview
To deduct the lies from the truth
Told to the world's judges

That I may walk that bridge
Laundered by foreign taxpayers
Before my birth

That I may see my picture
Not after the fact
With cut-offs and add-ons

That I may unsay the badly-said
In the construct of speech-saw puzzles
From a head tossed in ice

That I might undo the badly-done
In favour of my trash can
Far far away from here

That I may love with passion
Even the almost loveable
Not in puckish pools

That at the end of my journey
I might be remembered
Not for what I took but for what I gave

That I may truly earn
Forgiveness from above
In spite of hurdles before me

That I might speak the truth in love
And lick my love in truth
And keep hold of my lover

That I may war with warriors of the mind
That mind not afterword missiles thrown at random
To crush warriors that parade through muddied waters of
state

Love in time of Peace—Jubilee

The Invitation

You have checked in at the crossroads
Where hearts are poured out like wine
For the thirsty for laughter from the throats
And for the dancing of minds of the wise
Come... come... come and drink of this wine
And sign up for attendance at the meeting

This is Africa
This is *Matagelema*[14]
This is *Rogbane*[15]
This is the dream of the dreamers
Standing on battered and bleeding feet
Crawling on hardened knees and hands
Collecting whispers that holler
Whispers that announce the meeting of minds
Come... come from the cardinal points
And pass your whisper onto ears that are planted on the
ground

The stars are rising out of the ground
And the great Atlantic Ocean
Made greater by the priceless blood and bones of Africans
Is spreading with wings without end before our eyes
We are heaven-bound above the sky
The grass in the sky is growing on our ground
So we can wipe our feet on grass from the sky

---

[14] Matagelema is the name of a village in Mende country meaning "the end of
cat walk".

[15] *Rogbane* is the name of a village in Themnε country meaning "Where do we
meet?".

Here we kick open the drum of water
And it rains upon them below
Here there are no photographers
Because the angels are better diggers
Of girls that can slip into any camera

Come... our story has changed
Come... our names have changed
Come... come and rise with us
Come... come and dine with us
Come... come and dream with us

Come east... come west... come north... come south
This is where the cherished race must begin
This is where real conversations are started
With your face on the top of the mountain
There is no going back

Ayo Ayo Ayo[16]

Ayo ayo ayo ayo ayo!
Eeeeeey!
     Ayo ayo ayo!
     Eeeeeey!
         Ayo ayo!
            Eeeeeey!

The Great Muse has spoken,
So listen to the echo of his voice:
Listen now, and listen well!

     Hear me
     You *Matagelema*,
     Let us meet at *Rogbane*;
     The agenda is Siera Lyoa!

     Follow the line west of 1961,
     And you will find me;
     Follow the line east of 1961,
     And you will still find me.

     The nation is ripe
     For jubilee celebrations,
     With democracy
     In over-abundance.
     Love, joy and peace are faked,
     When there is famine
     In the land—my land!

---

[16] Ayo: language coined by some units of the police in Sierra Leone for celebration.

And there is famine in the land,
Until you are David to your Jonathan[17],
Or Muhammad[18] to your Book.

Hear me again
You over-prescribers of prosperity,
You under-prescribers of prosperity;
Hear me and hear me well!
I gave you an anthem
And I gave you a flag,
After I set you loose...
This is a well-earned jubilee for all who wink.

Did you see when the flower flowered
In the morning?
Its petals opened slowly to greet the sun,
And those who planted it
Saw the fruit long before it appeared.

The fruit appeared as fruit
Even for those who choked the flower,
With thorns from the outset.

This democracy has ripened for harvest;
This is why country boys have graduated into
city boys,
And the age-old bush
Has overgrown its boundary
And become a jargon on the lips of
democrats:

---

[17] Jonathan: David's bosom friend in the Bible (See 1 Samuel 20: 16-17)
[18] Prophet Muhammad, peace be upon him, is founder of the Muslim faith
and is said to have copied the Quoran as dictated by Allah (God).

So be it, so the Devil—that Old Boy,
May bow his head!

Now you can see a democrat
When a soldier hails the ballot,
Even though he has a bullet.
Or when the people fill their tummies
From adopted staple foods,
From the horizon—in defiance of pop foods.

Can't you see
That people stopped drinking spittle,
Because they now saw
That they lived on the banks of great waters
in plastic bags,
Which drowned them sometimes?

Can't you see
That the people now connect to power,
Since they own the power house?

Can't you see
That the long pregnancy of war
Delivered a new nation,
From the forest of thorns and wild beasts
That beat their chest,
Having caught the gift of transformation?

Can't you see
That the youths now hold the gavel
For things that touch on their lives?

Can't you see
That the tree of jubilee
Has a wide enough canopy to accommodate
Both birds of peace
And birds of prey?
But at the end of that,
It is the former
That shall sink the boat of the latter.

Can't you see
That the flowers of jubilee
Have opened
And are shooting towards the stars?

The clouds in the horizon
Shall only pour their shower of blessings
For the tenets of democracy to thrive:
Whether in a desert or on fertile ground
And the showers shall bring forth
Petals of rainbow colours—
Violet, indigo and blue of spirit,
Green for the evergreen heart,
Yellow, orange and red of the physical:
       Of religious tolerance,
       Of nationalism,
       Of integration,
       Of correct use of power,
       Of gender parity,
       Of lesser suffering…
And those who drop down from Mount
Ararat,
Being so much on the increase,

Shall whelm the virus of greed—
In money, healing and judgment houses.

And conjure maximum security,
In police and soldier ranks,
That Satan, that Old Boy, may bow.

And the Lungi bridge shall carry us to the side
of hope,
And the *Athens of West Africa*[19],
Shall wake up from sleep,
With no new references from the elite;
And deliver gains
From the shower of deliverance,
And Satan, that Old Boy will bow!

Can't you see
You have a right to say
What can help deliver this rain?
So say it, and let the Old Boy bow!

Say it! Say it!
And cast a prayer—in the year of jubilee:
No more bumpy roads. Amen!
No more *boloh-boloh*[20] in *attieke*[21]. Amen!
No more *peppeh-doctas*[22]. Amen!

---

[19] Sierra Leone was dubbed the *Athens of West Africa* as it became the
centre for higher learning in West Africa with the only university in tropical
Africa for a long time.
[20] *Boloh-boloh* is reference to phlegm as a result of *attieke*-selling women
digging their nose.
[21] *Attieke* (pronounced achekeh) is food made from cassava originating in
the Ivory Coast.

No more mercenary teachers. Amen!
No more *daka deke*[23] in business. Amen!
No more kangaroo courts in the workplace.
Amen!
No more *kukujumuku*[24]among the poor.
Amen!

So children may uncover their rights,
To help their parents know their rights.
And wives may stay from all-night prayers if
husbands slam a ban;
And dogs and roosters may stay in the bush,
And bears and deer may come to town.
So say it, in this year of jubilee!

Ayo!
Eeeeeeey!

---

[22] *Peppeh-docta* is the name given to unqualified doctors causing deaths in the country.
[23] *Daka deke* business is referring to corrupt practices in business e.g. 419.
[2424] *Kuku-jumuku* in Mende means running with corruption or deceptive practices among gangs.

Sallay Kama Sallay[25]

Sallay kama sallay!
Bosway! Bosway!

Sallay kama sallay!
Bosway! Bosway!

Sallay kama sallay!
Bosway! Bosway!

Palm fronds in the sun
Have catapulted the earth dirt into the eyes,
In Wilkinson Road—in broad daylight:
As if to construct anger and rage
In slow-moving cars,
In Wilkinson Road—in broad daylight!

But no!
There is beauty in the horizon
Shining like sea in the road,
Wilkinson Road—in the year of jubilee:

And the blast of laughter from old cars
Will level with speed
The mountain of wastepaper journals
Flying out of car windows,
In Wilkinson Road—a road changing direction by the hour:
The Chinese[26] gift of road jigsaws

---

[25] *Sallay Kama Sallay*: Mende rendition of the English 'Challenge common challenge; and the response is *Bosway Bosway*, which means 'both ways both ways'—in the face of a great task the chorus of this pronouncement favours success/breakthrough.

To Salone.

And control of the road,
Of everything;
Is sometimes lost to cars and heedless headless drivers,
Who fail to see the beauty of the road ahead.

It is hoped that jubilee will breed joy,
When enemies of progress
Shall seal their lips and pockets
And be converted into friends of progress;

And we will forget to play the game of chess,
At the violet hour:
And the expression *man butu man wach*[27]
Or *Dem say Bailor Barrie*
Yu se Davidson Nicol?[28]
Shall be deleted from our memory cards
And in a couple of months
The women will drop their catwalk
For a salute from those men
Who salute women's hips:
And such men will now see the grace
That gave birth to precious hips.

And in a couple of months,
There will be water supply

---

[26] The Chinese won the contract for constructing Wilkinson Road.
[27] *Man butu man wach:* A Krio expression meaning one person is waiting
to ride on the mistake of another.
[28] *Dem say Bailor Barrie yu se Davidson Nicol:* A Krio expression meaning,
the most important thing at this time is money (represented by Bailor
Barrie) and not education (represented by Davidson Nicol).

For all on the edges of great waters—in the city;
And in villages where villagers drown the waters,
In the old old forests.

Give us a couple of months
And Bumbuna[29] will begin to visit certain towns and villages,
Before travelling abroad for foreign exchange.

And in a couple of months,
The differently-abled persons
Will forget the farmhouses of the past,
Where they were abandoned for other gains.

And in a couple of months
The mothers will show greater care for their babies,
And still be in the fifty-fifty game,
In honour of precious deadlines.

And in a couple of months,
All NGOs will honestly justify
Their income in line with the work they say they do.
In Wilkinson Road.
      Oh Salone,
What a price you pay for development!

And now even now,
No new sect will filter itself into the system,
And say they are a Church or Mosque:
For fire shall fall

---

[29] Bumbuna village is where the waterfall is that is supplying hydro electricity to the country.

On Churches and Mosques that visit from hell,
And save the nation from obscurantism;
Of isms from all schisms.

Give us a couple of months,
And the newly-found black gold
Will not displace the weak from the land that they love,
But honour them with well-deserving rewards:
At the dawn of engagement…

And the new MP[30] shall love to write his name,
In consonance with their *alma mater*,
To prompt them—before the violet hour.

Yes! Yes! Yes!
This rhythm of progress must go on,
Till late comers report for duty!

If independence means severance from dependence in a
new jacket,
Then this must go on!

If God did make men and women equal,
With a mandate to reproduce their kind,
Taking cognizance of population size,
Then this must go on.

If the head boys and head girls will not betray the nation,
In the year of jubilee,
Then this must go on!

---

[30] MP: Member of Parliament

If parents will not wear their children's trousers,
To distract celebrants,
In the year of jubilee,
Then this must go on!

If the academic giants will not sell their birthrights,
For a plate of *foofoo*[31],
In the year of jubilee,
Then this must go on!

If the *Athens of West Africa*
Will wake up from sleep,
In this precious year of jubilee,
Then this must go on!

If civil servants will stop dreaming
Of *usay dem tay kaw na de i go it gras*[32],
Then this must go on!

If godly leaders will stop fighting each other
From corners of unholy testimonies,
Then this must go on!

If black friends of state
Will stop taking black messages to State House,
Like those black birds in the violet hour,
Then this must go on!

If the tribes ever come together,

---

[31] *Foofoo* is the name given to a pasty food made from cassava by the Creoles.

[32] *Usay dem tay kaw na de I go it gras:* A Krio expression meaning the cow must eat from the grass within its tether.

And forget their tribal tethers,
In a new dance involving all,
Then this must go on!

If citizens still in chain
Can allow themselves to be liberated,
In the dawn of the jubilee,
Then this must go on!

If students will heed the thought that cheating in exams
Is a wrong start for the workplace,
Then this must go on!

This nation needs a potion
That will make dry bones come alive,
A potion that will make tasty flesh become sour—
In the mouths of vultures;
So those vultures can fly away to the land of no return.

We have the potion that will add flesh and spirit and life
To Wallace Johnson,[33]
Who will come with a pen filled with blood,
From cowards, to rewrite our constitution.

This nation has that potion
That will kill loneliness born to marriages,
Contracted in holy houses.

So let the fire fall and shake everything bone,
Let the fire fall and soften hearts of stone:

---

[33] Isaac Theophilus Akuna Wallace-Johnson was a famous Sierra Leonean trade unionist that worked closely with Kwame Nkrumah of Ghana. His pen was very powerful.

And unnamed roses will salute the rising stars,
In the maturing star of a nation.

Sallay kama sallay!
Bosway! Bosway!

I stooped by the Nile for a Wash

Chupoon… chupoon
Chupoon chupoon chupoon
I stooped by the Nile for a wash
All the waters from the desert
Had headed there in search of fish
So I washed off the dust of the years
Real dust since fifty years ago

But anachronistic practices
Formed a magnetic field for my fingers
And dark tribal traditions stuck like glue
To my brain and blood
Chupoon… chupoon
Chupoon chupoon chupoon
Colourful brain and colourful blood all the way

Seven times seven years plus one
I went for the Jubilee wash
Chupoon… chupoon
Chupoon chupoon chupoon
I could quote every good book from cover to cover
But the mummies gave up on me
They saw that my heart was un-washable

I drank from the cup of the Pharaohs
And accepted fifty of their slaves
So my land could become the new Egypt
 Chupoon… chupoon
Chupoon chupoon chupoon
I took a wash and called myself a Pharaoh
But the Pharaoh could not enter my blood

There were lions all over giving shape to my mountains
But I lost my own lion heart
When the lion let me loose for a run
Chupoon... chupoon
Chupoon chupoon chupoon
I locked the door of development for my land
And gave the key to an untraceable monkey

No one won the gold for this first lap
But all were given the chance for a second chance
And this wash in the Nile
Chupoon... chupoon
Chupoon chupoon chupoon
Will send me home with Pharaoh's hate for fake
partnerships
And regroup nostalgia with anathema issues

And so Nkrumah and Lincoln among others
Volunteered to wash me this time
 Chupoon... chupoon
Chupoon chupoon chupoon
And they chorused *better late than not try*
And the earlier water of my washing
Flowed downstream in search of fish from desert waters

But tell me who fished here before Pedro
Or who got marooned here before the Maroons
Who depended on whom before independence
These thoughts put me to sleep and wake me from sleep

I just need an anniversary wash
Chupoon... chupoon

Chupoon chupoon chupoon
And then I'd cleanse my thoughts from sticky trash
In the road

The New Salone Leone

They say as they always do
That the Salone Leone
Of the Seventies
Died with the Seventies

But you know as well as I do
That the Salone Leone
Of the Seventies
Never lay claim on immortality
In the face of fatalities
As dark as the Seventies
As stark as the Seventies

But that was in the rains
When the ground was wet for growing notes
As one might grow Rice or Coconut
From the wet soil
Of Rutile or Gold or Diamond

Yet we still have the rains
As we do the dries
As we do the vibes

Sure enough
The Salone Leone will grow taller
Than the tallest coconut tree
On your heart

If your heart is wet soil
Even in the absence of rain

Yes when it pours
As it is about to pour
From the new new sky
With a song on development and transformation
A rainbow from your heart

Indeed
In the new jazz of wet and dry
You are the Salone Leone
Shooting above the sky

back to you

your mouth drips of sugar
in promises
yet to be fulfilled
even though refilled
with judgment fair or unfair
in and out of trust
in and out of trust

your eyes speak more than your mouth
those looks good or bad
blow volumes
in a non-speaking contest
i am giving them back to you
giving them back to you
back to you

your ears are reading too much
yet they write little
in suspicion of writers
so they bottle up
what belongs to others
why not open up
you better open up

Love for Love's Sake

Forgiveness

Forgiven—I have been forgiven.
To forgive—let me be a giver,
And to give—let me be a loser,
And to lose—let me be a winner.

I'm sorry—let someone say I'm sorry.
I'm sorry—'cause someone else was sorry.
They're sorry—so we too must be sorry.
We're sorry—so we all are the winners!

You're happy—and that's why I am happy.
I'm happy—and that's why they are happy.
They're happy—and that's why all are happy.
All are happy—and that's why all are winners!

Love Conversation

M:[34] Since I became your spouse the snob of society became meaningless.

W:[35] Of course, you ought to know, I voted you my President.

M: The trees stopped dropping their leaves.
W: Yes, I gave you a garden of evergreens.

M: But the birds have not stopped singing.
W: Because my griots serve you with perpetual interest.

M: Witness now my name on every lip in the country.
W: No surprise! I jammed their wavelength with my broadcasts.

M: I never went hungry.
W: Not since I became your daily bread.

M: Never went thirsty either.
W: How can you when my forest well has been reserved for you only?

M: Nor have I been lonely.
W: No darling, I gave you a piece of me to take everywhere.

---

[34] "M" is for Man
[35] "W" is for Woman

M: Even when I bought no jewels for you?

W: Honey, what can be more precious than your teeth in smiles?

M: So you see why I waited for you?

W: But was there another option for a God-appointed waiter?

M: And our love has not ended in the mouth.

W: No! I even feel it in my phalanges and frame.

M: See how you promoted me—the Easter lily of the plains!

W: And so have you promoted me the apple being chewed inside your ears!

M: You are a garden of roses of the colours that matter to the heart!

W: You are a bundle of harvesters that know what matters to the heart!

M: Your garments smell of Paris in the evening!

W: Your lips taste of chocolate from La Côte d'Ivoire!

M: Your two breasts are the torches that give my body direction!

W: You are the palm tree I was waiting to climb for nourishing oil!

M: Can heaven be different from what I know?

W: What you allow me to share is a foretaste of heaven.

M: So, *for better for worse?*
W: I'll be the code for your conduct.

M: *For richer for poorer?*
W: I'll be your tax collector.

M: *In sickness and in health?*
W: I will drug you on.

M: Is this how we pray today?
W: And everyday.

M/W: Aaaaah men!

God Is Posh

god is posh in the ghettoes
where trash is flash
of posh or purse
for a life wary of lush

god is ape in the forest
where games of doubt
are plagued by meshy minds
tried for angles of fuss

god is dream at home
where security is segregation
of measurement and hope
in the subplots of bonds

god is posh with poshy minds
that would throw only leftovers
of development riddles
toward the poor from riddled reigns

god is sold by priests that peep
torn blinds for chances of gold
once sold as the earnest
of development index in heaven

god is posh as posh is lush
for minds of buoyant flavours of taste
only tasted by the favoured
through invitations to parties by the posh

god is dreamer and foolish
for making man MAN
man is dreamer and clever
for making GOD god

I Married a Sheep

I married a sheep
After my wolfish tricks
I taught the sheep some leaping
Who never would obey
Me too I walked the sheep way
Though a hard gait to play

The day began with a wolfish sheepish
laughter
And yet did end
With a sheepish wolfish cry

Right now the sheep a wolfish sheep
Beside me a sheepish wolf
For us both a gentle gait would strike
To spite the shying mind

The Eye-less God

The eye-less God needs your eyes
that use two lenses,
or more:
That he might see...
Will you let him?

The ear-less God needs your ears
that use two eardrums,
or more:
That he might hear...
Will you let him?

The nose-less God needs your nose
that uses two holes,
or more:
That he might smell...
Will you let him?

The mouth-less God needs your mouth
that uses two lips,
or more:
That he might speak...
Will you let him?

The arm-less God needs your arms
that use two hands,
or more:
That he might touch...
Will you let him?

The leg-less God needs your legs
that use two feet,
or more:
That he might move...
Will you let him?

The heart-less God needs your heart
that uses two pipes,
or more:
That he might feel...
Will you let him?

The all-mind God would have your mind,
That uses two heads,
Or more:
That he might think...
If you let him.

God the Poet

God is my greatest Poet
Because
He nearly bursts my eardrums
When He drums the words
I AM
I fix the metres of the world
And keep spreading the rhythm
Of my stars
Period

A letter to a pen friend

Your name in my pen is all that spells love,
Yet in that pain could be found a dodging dove.

In my pen there might be war-backing words,
But not a blood-letting demon with swords.

I write then you write, you write then I write;
I writhe over culture that spills the spite.

The postmark has invited forgiveness,
Over such pregnancy of barrenness.

And patient Pascal recommends the wait,
Over matters of word-full heavyweight.

A thoughtful reply is the retainer
Of an advocate for a good dinner.

Then the first chance for the meeting faces,
Declares rights to a deserving embrace.

If such were to fall in the space between us,
Then let us embrace as if on a love cross.

No Need to Say Farewell

No need to say farewell
When the next stop is just fresh water on the ground
You could drink our water again
Moments after that farewell

Someone may take your place
Someone indeed should
But someone may not give your smile
Over doubts that must be cleared

Someone may flag your queries
Someone may flag your signature
Someone may flag the hours you gained
Someone may flag the hours you lost

Never mind the references on you
Which take their queues from green-eyed monsters
With own-made typescript so sketched in
For the office to feed and grow from

But history will spit out the poison
Picked up from reference books on you
That chokes the speed of commitment
And all will get to know you for who you were

A Letter to my Child at Eighteen

My dear child
I tiptoed to crack eighteen
As you dance to this spent teen
Some your age fall short of dance
Nonetheless they had their chance

So mark stones on this long road
Which some tread with measured load
In their way they greet with hurt
Yet some wait to tease with love
Know the case and name the place

Share this thought also from polls
That man not God names the fools
Those who rise with time unnamed
Shake well the hand of the named
So be a friend beyond eyes
To see some tails in the lies

So move to stand in the light
So that night may not alight
But if they step on your toes
Thank God they awoke the bones

Talk to silence after noise
And reject all uncouth joys
End laughter in belly shakes
Start weeping in belly shakes
Those who are noble inside
Are double noble outside

Flash your light on sleeping stars
And be a star that stations stars
Employ yourself to look at depths
The actual sea is in its depths
You are a Queen to friends if…
You are a Beggar to them if…

Look at Success their good friend
Look at Failure their good fiend
Your songs are good if inspired
But do not sing for vampires
Sing as blest before you land

Orate this again and rise

Breaking News from New Orleans

Breaking news of Noah's flood
For eyes that wink and ears that tingle
Is bound to break hearts
Is bound to break bridges

The night that fell defied your west and my east
Though night only for angels but a bite for the beast
Surprised by a wailing wind
On the shores of New Orleans

Soothsaying as an art
Has been clinched by forecasters
Of rain and wind and flood
For rolling out the night

Beware Honey
Bells of night may ring again
To wake the sleepers of day
If only they can rise from sleep

I can hear your cry
The great wind brought it to me
In the middle of my sleep
Now a shrill scream from your bloodless bones

Like the cry here
Your voice bounces around my neighbourhood
And they regret that I regret
That I was so given and gone

I can recall our last summer
Around the kissing gate
On another plate of love
The farewell only meant always present

It was good we tried to be good
Not promising the spacewalk
Or the catwalk for eyes
That pop up for television screens

But did Katrina steal you from me
In envy of the love song that put me to sleep
With you standing on top of a friendly roof
Still whispering my name with that song

Katrina might make a show of you
And grant you accolades for cinematic positions
From a culture of shows
But you will never ever shy away from love

The Dance of the Nude

The picture on my son's wall violates my visit:
The blues from the wild west with four legs.
In the nude they dance on the wall:
I can't guess when that drawing entered his poll,
Entered my son's poll,
To find a place on the western wall of his parlour.

I thought my culture was violated upon first sight,
But when I entered the guest room I felt I was raped.
Indeed the nude dance started way back,
When his father said don't misbehave or I'll send you
away...
From decency... Away...
From heaven to hell, from this Ca to that Ca.

And the day I stepped outside to view the sea,
Four legs danced on the porch like they came down from
the wall:
Four human legs of equal shape and length as those on the
wall.
And there too the walls were loaded so much,
With the nude parade so much
As coming from abroad like my learned son.

I am a prisoner of conscience within these walls,
And my youth-age visits me with a raised axe:
So I ask, what did I deprive you of in those days?
I denied you cinema going in good faith my love,
But not study time my love,
So I draw a clean landscape not a dirty mindscape.

But here this returnee has chained our landscape
And introduced multifaceted hills to the plain,
Thereby raping even the breast that gave him bread.
But what will weeping do to a drunken son in the nude?
Only sharpen his pencil of nude!
But that new drawing will not violate my eyes, never!

The Peace of Christmas

This fully spirited rendition
Of tranquilizers,
Packaged by innocence—in a manger,
In a manger,
Has surprised the hungry and the angry with peace.

But down the road in years ahead,
Mary Magdalene waits,
With many heads,
That will settle
For peace not dreamed of;
Yet cares less who cares,
And would follow her new-found dream
To view a Roman cross.

As for today, Father Christmas
Has chosen to be a toy
To countless children—a celebrity god;
Tantalizing them with gifts—not in a manger,
Not in a manger,
But packaged with superficiality
For the anger sleeping into hunger,
In the ambivalence of ambiance.

Accept my offer of
Peace for Christmas—not on a platter,
Not on a platter,
Neither packaged in the superfluity of moments
But the simplicity of purposeful humanity;
To be sung by shepherds

Who long for morning light.

The peace of Christmas.
　　　The peace of Christmas.
　　　　　The peace of Christmas.
　　　　　　　The peace of Christmas.
　　　　　The peace of Christmas.
　　　The peace of Christmas.
The peace of Christmas.

Silence Please

Your voice bounces through the building,
From bottom to top:
It hit my eardrums;
On the seventh floor,
And deadened my brain.

If you joined the choir,
You would sing bass;
But this building,
Opts for another voice –
        SILENCE!

Will you cast your vote?

Birthday Greeting

Out of sheer love
In the desert of love play
How can I say I love you
And go Scot-free

Neither in a birthday cake
Cut out there on a love lake
Can a boat rock a toast
And make you go Scot-free

I will rest my pen
Just to raise my voice
And holler the distance to silence
For love play in a sentence

Happy birthday honey

The Song of a Sheep
(based on Psalm 23)

The Lord is my Captain, I shall not drift.

He assigns me a quiet cabin,
Speaks to me through the sea shells,
And my soul now has a heart.
His name in my ears is a call to righteous steps.
Yes, His name is a command.

Though I am overwhelmed by shocks,
I will dread no intrusions;
For you are beside me,
Whispering soft counsel,
So I cannot be impeached.

Your blessings come upon me like rain,
And even my enemies call me great.
My shower cap gives way to your anointing touch,
And my cup of oil overflows.

Surely I shall remain blest
All the days of my life,
And I will stay
In my God-given cabin,
Forever.

A Teacher's Prayer

God protect me from myself
The cliff of my ignorance
Pretends joy beyond the edge
But I see the dangerous cracks
In bottles of foolhardiness
O Lord save me from myself

Sometimes I feel I'm wisest
Even in my ignorance
I will mark time like Steve Hawking
Or shake on stage like Shakespeare
Yet hurtle down like Hate's spear
Lord protect me from myself

Sometimes I spit spurious answers
Good cause for calling friends fools
I open my amphora
But not a millionth degree
Of your consciousness have I
Please protect me from myself

God protect me from myself
Let me know I sleep in you
Let me know I wake in you
Let me know I move in you
And without you I am damned
Lord set me free from myself

Thank you Lord for loving me
My excesses notwithstanding

Stupidities against life
Mislead those who follow me
And I'm mocked with my Nation
Save us from idiosyncrasies

God save this State from those vain elite
Save her children from bad dreams
Save her parents from negligence
Save her friends from bigotry
May new wisdom shine on board
Where her people peddle Word

God I know I am a fool
Molded to be a good tool
For pursuing excellence
But even as fool I fail
To serve your benign designs
Dear Lord save me from myself. AMEN

Holy Saturday

Cryptically labyrinthine:
A much needed haven from the hell of the world,
For the trio at this point in time.
Their march was unto sanity as if from insanity.
This special group for the Lord's workshop,
Needed a retreat to retreat from fishing,
To a more profitable fishing vocation.
For a quieter Saturday city than ours.
Than ours!
So, where is Peter
And where is James,
And where is John?

I can understand a bout of smallpox or chickenpox or
cowpox
That can take one to a hide-out hospital
Beyond the knowledge of friends
Beyond the knowledge of the king
Beyond the knowledge even of one's spouse

Where is Peter?
Peter went on sabbatical
To attend a short course on fishing:
Soon enough he should be able to use fishing boats,
Or become a fishing professor in a fishing college.
I don't mean for fishing mobile phones
At PZ[36], no.
He will not take a PhD in fishing, no.

---

[36] PZ: Paterson Zochonis, a popular junction named after a defunct mall in
Freetown.

He is aware that the fishing business is into billions per year,
And he is going for that...
But will he last there?

Where is James?
He went to plan a coup.
No longer keen on sitting beside God
It is okay if he has power here:
Power to command as Grand Commander of the Armed
Forces;
Power to shout like thunder, the voice of God;
Power to kick people around like football;
And power to sleep through international conferences.
Jesus left a wrong notion of power:
Look at him parading in hell displaying power,
And yet his men are looking for power
That is neither in heaven nor in hell.
Rather than feed the hungry,
He is talking to demons.
Rather than heal the sick,
He is taking a lost and found key from the underworld.

But why should James not go for elections?
At least he died for his faith.
Oh *Mother of God,*
Pray for us sinners that we may honour our democracy,
And stand in elections when we become redundant,
Or resign from our posts when we become redundant,
Pray for us sinners, now and the hour of our death.
> *now and the hour of our death*
> *now and the hour of our death*
> *now and the hour of our death*

But we died before now long long ago:
Remember the loss of the railway track;
Remember the Green Revolution that happened in hotels;
Remember the many coups d'état;
Remember the farce of the ABC[37] on our character;
Remember, remember, and remember!
Oh Mother of God,
Pray for us sinners,
Now and the hour of our new death.
Where is John?
He went in to master writing:
He wrote about everything
Including love,
Including warnings about hell,
And real kingdom matters.
He became a real journalist,
Preaching louder than John the Baptist his former master.
He so mastered the call of journalism
That Journalists after him, instead of Pastors,
Have their heads displayed on platters.

Including love—
        Love that a Pastor got wrong when he eloped with
his catechist's wife
        Love that a sportsman got wrong when he took
performance enhancing drugs
And warnings about hell—
        Hell that is misunderstood in daily conversations
        Hell that is not known at the fireside
And real Kingdom matters—

---

[37] ABC: 'Attitudinal and Behavioral Change,' name of the office set up by
the President after the celebration of the Jubilee.

Not the kingdoms created by Bishops
No, not the Kingdom of empire builders

We should join the fasting squad,
On today
Today being Holy Saturday,
A day taken from the world
A day given to the Lord!

St. Valentine's Day

St. Valentine's Day never hit me
Like the day I got married:
A little drizzle and then shine
In April—that famous month.

My eyes caught her hip
At a floral shop on St. Valentine's Day.
I don't really know
If she wore those trousers for my eyes
So that when she stooped to pick up her bouquet,
My eyes caught the path
dividing the lobes on her tail equally.

I said to her, 'Lady, you disgust me.
I hate you!'
She said in return, 'This flower is for an anonymous friend.
Can you have it?'
'But you have not hit me
Like the day of my marriage.
A little drizzle, and then shine.
This February afternoon is too hot
With you in my eyes. So I hate you!
I just wish it rained right here!'
She nearly converted me you know,
I almost fell for her:
But her type of trousers,
not my chunk of roasted cassava
Dumped and left me in a ditch.

I have not been to America
But I know they are too civil to be that.

So now I want American friends,
That would write to me
In their President's English,
>   And wear her kind of trousers,
>   And wear her kind of jacket,
>   And wear her kind of shirt,
>   And wear her kind of necktie.
Maybe I should fly to America,
On the wings of an eagle.

I must go to America when I can!
They say Americans carry guns everywhere
Because they have enemies everywhere.
I hear we too will start our parade of guns—
After manufacturing our numerous enemies:
>   Guns to the farm house,
>   Guns to the market place,
>   Guns to the classroom,
>   And of course guns to the office.
We could start becoming our own enemies,
To take our own lives when angry with God,
Sorry I mean when angry with our spouses:
Because guns will be for us the easy way out.
Yes, I must go to America when I can.
Anyhow I can.
Anywhere I can.
And I believe I can!

Victoria Falls Again

I came I saw and was stoutly conquered
By a river with a gap in its middle
A big bowl cut in the earth as if it knew

Those worldlings would come for a shower
 on its banks

I came here when the rain killed cameras
And sentenced cheap mobile phones to silence
With human voices harassed and embarrassed
By the vexed spirit of Victoria Falls

Even the rainbow is cowered and bent
In apologies to Ma Zambezi
Who fumed dews of blessings on its bent back
In downloads and uploads without a fee

I am puzzled by sudden presences
Of nations jumping out of anxious beds
To watch the rainbow drink water like fish
Ready for the swim when not playing prey

Oh Ma Zambezi still in habit mode
See how you spit your fume like puff adder
When did you learn to paint your strangers so
To make them fall on Livingstone in stone
Did you spit on Livingstone like that
When he sought for refuge in your bushes
How dare you make him bend to drink water

103

Water from below and water from above

That furtive Livingstone had tripped
On a rainbow under his feet
And now has a word of welcome for pals
Who come but hardly ever stay to hide

Love as Continuum of Communion:

Situations, Self, Souls and Saints

Born Again—I am

Human born—I am
Birthday known—I do
Live on earth—oh yes
But does it matter?

Celebrity made—I am
Celebrity unmade—I am
Are there options—oh yes
But does it matter?

Spirit Born—I am
Angel natured—I am
Am I known—oh yes
But does it matter?

Born again—I am
Conference speaker—I am
Do I drum it—oh yes
But does it matter?

Professional gossip—I am
Professional thief—I am
Do people know it—oh yes
But does it matter?

Church Agba—I am
Moneyed Shepherd—I am
Does God know it—oh yes
But does it matter?

Do you love me—maybe?
Do I love you—maybe?
Does God love me—oh yes
But does it matter?

The Gift She Gave

Passing this world is a gift
She gave it oh yes she gave it
By hanging a bomb round her waist
To shatter the waists of wasters
So that paralysis too
Is a gift that has come with boos

Strange gift with a strange pattern
Rocking the stage for strange grabs
In the tents of halleluiahs
On the pellets of hurrahs
The gift that has come thus far
With dynamites unstoppable

Did you see her pass your way
Did she wave a kerchief there
Did you hear her mighty praises
Of things you never can embrace
Her lullabies killed their pains
Strange rain that quenched new fires of farms

Elegy on the Death of a University Don
(To the Revd. Dr. Leslie E. T. Shyllon—on his written request before death that a poem be done in place of a sermon by this author—Friday 20th November 2009)

You stars that sell the gloomy late evening news
Willing harbingers!
Have declared untold sleeplessness
On the eternal legal instance of nature and time fleeting
time
To search into the night for truth in rumours
Did the summer leaves that took the Fall pass
Actually fall to the ground and turn into ash
This tale must not be sold in Freetown only
Where the Venetian palate is on top
And the tongue *non est* in battle
This account is with the seller who died
Instantly after the big bang event
You who specialise in telling tall tales
Who know of stars and their names and their age
When they are active or uninteresting
When they are living or dead
What is the sealing or ceiling on your knowledge here
What would his wife of those many years say
Or his children who still go by his word
Or his friends who communed with him daily
Or the students who in search of knowledge
Searched him daily to drink from the water of Lees
Or congregations that grappled with the methods
Of salvation for mankind
In the name of acknowledged religion
What has become an avowed misnomer
With friends spitting brimstone at friends

And the man would interject *et tu Brute*
Then stood Caesar to throw the dart at Brutus
Then fell Brutus to mark the start of war
But was there a seminar for students
On truth in the Chapel or polyclinic
Of how the *hoi polloi* are displaced
By the anointed intelligentsia
On the Altar of greed and sadism
No more than the Church historian can tell
And the itinerant, surreptitious
Vulture-like doves will come in their numbers
To flank the aisle with their gowns and skirts and rompers
In carefully graded sympathy
For me I am left to chew upon this truth
I have seen tears
But let compassion be showered from heaven
Yes passion in gentle drops on all heroes
For all are heroes in the arena
All are champions in the game of death
Who started dying the very day of birth
But did I hear you say he died
How can they die who hoist the flag of truth
I mean truth that flies and truth that hides
As long as other scholars feed on it
Kings, Noble Men, Entrepreneurs
And Seraphim All
As long as healers daydream by it
As long as Shepherds find their sheep by it
Let that passion fall with speed on them all

...on them all
...on them all
...on them all
...on them all
...on them all
...on them all
...on them all

Tonie French, (OW)

Did I hear you say she died

Can they die who live in songs
Of waves that never never die
She cannot die who left her name
In microphones that will not break

If you hold that then John Akar too
Who tethered her to microphones
And gave her tips on vocal laws
Is good as gone or worse than straws

Or

You stage stars
Do you agree
Her light went out with that sad word
That quaked the calm and stopped the waves
As in wake of Dele's case

Oh no… Oh no… Oh no… Oh no…
She lives to us and lives to God
Whose catholic spirit knew no bounds
For God and Salone in the rounds

Queen Tonie the First
Of Kingdom Busy
Of the Order of the Waves (OW)…

Eh eh… did I hear you say she died

The Journey of the Loner
(To Wiltshire Samuel Bomotilewa Johnson, Ph.D)

Tapered trust
Taunted and tried
In the wars of the world
What you won
Was long willed
By the wilier of winners
You are just another package of dreams
Packed by a world of non-dreamers
The stars you set on fire
From the chemistry of speech
Will stay lighted and brilliant
Except they choose to be miscreant
As missing links in their missions

Oh Salone the loner
You have just packed another loner
Another packet of dreams
Because you failed to see the dreams
Because they shone not as you deemed
Maybe you lost your very steam

Oh my brother
The insoluble soul of Salone
Seal of the seers
Go get your laurels
Only be guided not to miss
The lane of laurel takers
Lured only by the crown
In the hand of the laurel giver
The conversations you posited here

Will converse for as long as you crack on
About which Americans or Russians spied on heaven
About where God sat when He made the sad things
About the darker things that men dream of dashing their
kind
Things that lions never dream of doing their kind
With a look at the verse in vogue
The spirit you gave birth to
Will give birth to your kind
But over there yes over there
Our quarters may be close
And the conversation will continue
Just maybe
Only maybe

The Princess of My Heart
(For Princess Diana)

The Princess of my heart indeed
Courted the heart of death
And cut a canal for fresh tears
When she hit the eyes of sunlight
That hit my blind at dawn

This path of printed pages raw
How royalty trod it for gain
But my lone star did spot the sign
Of printed minds as well
Who had to paint the Paint

The phenomenal race course
Has bitter gold to give
No cheering stadia fans
To a game of non-starters
Where God Himself is Ref

The Princess of the New Empire
How can you say they killed her
Who did what and when and where and how
The underdogs bear me out
Her life is red ink there

This full moon day has filled my eyes
With water of salt so deep
My Queen will ride into tomorrow
Her Saviour calls her home
Where angels praise and pray

The bridge that tripped her soul from sole
Robbed her of all she had
Consuming her love in anger bent
Herself a swinging bridge
Upon pent-up pen pals

My Tears Will Hang in There
(For Cyril Patrick Foray)

My tears will hang in there until I stand
Where I stood endlessly knocking knocking
The knocking sounded round the house but oh
No one responded with a yes or no

My tears will hang in there until I sit
Where I sat listing wisdom wisdom
The wisdom of the years fanned my poor brain
But brain cracking sometimes leads to the drain

I sat there just as CP too sat there
I sat there pondering dreaming musing
My tears will hang in there until I bounce
And touch the door and chair of remembrance

My tears will hang in there where history broods
Over the brood of a new millennium
Brash taciturnity salutes the state
With statelessness juggling on the state slate

Let CP go and yet let CP stay
What's there in going that's not in staying
Though some go by air and others by sea
They will all arrive and that's their plate of rice

My tears will hang in there though not to hang
Hang a drop per second of his days done
Divide those by words that dropped from his lips
He must have healed millions by way of drips

117

So I raise my hands and head to heaven
To steal the peace from the pique in the pie
Let CP go and yet let CP stay
A day will dawn when history becomes pay

Hector Pietersons
(Written after visiting the Museum in Soweto on 26th May 2006)

Hector Pietersons—name or idea
Pulls the string on my tears
Boiling at source to shower on museums
In the jungle of pain I am poured
Like the due of the morning
There are unsung songs in here
Pulling on the song of my tongue
Wetted by tears—this time of night
But the morning will come
And they'll know the unknown singer
In the morning after the mourning
They rise every day following the night
I have seen them rise with a word
That message is immortal so much more
And I have a call to rise—alone
Or with them—each time they rise

Great Hero of Battles
(To Tom Cauuray)

Great hero of battles,
Thanks for sharing your epitaph
In Deuteronomic proportions:
We shall inscribe the same on the stones of our hearts,
Stones that might not be broken;
By anger from the Muse's Lieutenant,
In answer to unkind questions.

Great hero of battles,
You have seen it all,
And said it all,
In righteous indignation:
We shall rebuild this nation in answer to your voice;
Before it falls into the bottomless pit,
Before it translates into a monster.

Great hero of battles,
Your baritone voice hits the boisterous eardrum
Of the whistler from superficial realms:
Hard hard talk of un-talked talks,
Brisk and firm in love's domain,
Tender yet tough in hate's terrain;
Though truth and untruth may soar in pain.
Great hero of battles,
There must be a destination for you,
With Bishop Chicken-out—the servant of my bicycle:
So move on to the end of battles,
But not the end of thinking,
For answers to many many questions,
To which no one should guess the answers.

Taataa Uncle Tata
(To Tatafway Tumoe)

He was always on his feet:
Leaving,
      Believing,
      Arriving;
But never returning!
 When he did,
It was to another town,
      Another family,
      Anther friend,
      Another address.

So we say taataa Uncle Tata.
Whenever you come back;
Forgive the new town,
      The new family,
      The new friend,
      The new address.

We did our best:
      For town to stay,
For family to stay,
For friend to stay,
For address to stay;
But aah yaah, please forgive!
Forgive partings
That patronized patriotism.
That begged the question of poor returns
In black and white.
Forgive:
Forgive the Salone way of saying farewell.

121

A hundred years today
The dogs will bark their old shouts,
The birds will sing their old tunes,
But the people will be singing new tunes
From Salone, the Olympic Star for Tunes.

A hundred years today,
The children will be asking:
taataa Uncle Tata
But why did you leave?
We'll all be there someday:
To wave a greeting,
Or wave a farewell
from the other side.

If you please!

Printed in the United States
By Bookmasters